Praise for *Girl on an Altar*

'An important new play by one of Ireland's greatest playwrights.' *Irish Times*

'Theatrical storytelling of the highest order . . . Carr's language shimmers in [the actors'] mouths like fire . . . an intense, intimate epic.' *Daily Express*

'The writing brings a cool rigour to the extremity of the events and emotions in the spotlight: Carr's text is full of wonderful, muscular poetry.' *Financial Times*

'Carr translates the trauma-ridden women of Greek tragedies exceptionally . . . [Her] narrative skills are enthralling.' *Broadway World*

Girl on an Altar

Marina Carr was brought up in County Offaly. A graduate of University College Dublin, she has written extensively for the theatre. She has taught at Villanova, Princeton, and is currently Associate Professor in the School of English, Dublin City University. Awards include the Susan Smith Blackburn Prize, the Macaulay Fellowship, the E. M. Forster Prize from the American Academy of Arts and Letters, and the Windham Campbell Prize. She lives in Dublin with her husband and four children.

MARINA CARR

Girl on an Altar

faber

First published in 2022
by Faber and Faber Limited
The Bindery, 51 Hatton Garden
London, EC1N 8HN

This edition published in 2023

Typeset by Brighton Gray
Printed and bound in the UK by CPI Group (Ltd), Croydon CR0 4YY

A CIP record for this book
is available from the British Library

978-0-571-37875-3

Printed and bound in the UK on FSC® certified paper in line with our continuing
commitment to ethical business practices, sustainability and the environment.
For further information see faber.co.uk/environmental-policy

Girl on an Altar was first performed at the Kiln Theatre, London, on 19 May 2022, with the following cast:

Clytemnestra Eileen Walsh
Agamemnon David Walmsley
Cassandra Nina Bowers
Aegisthus Daon Broni
Cilissa Kate Stanley-Brennan
Tyndareus Jim Findley

Director Annabelle Comyn
Designer Tom Piper
Lighting Designer Amy Mae
Composer and Sound Designer Philip Stewart
Video Designer Will Duke
Casting Director Julia Horan CDG
Movement Director /
 Intimacy Director Ingrid Mackinnon
Voice and Dialect Coach Danièle Lydon
Costume Supervisor Isobel Pellow
Assistant Director Jessica Mensah

The play was revived at the Abbey Theatre, Dublin, on 8 July 2023, with the following changes:

Cassandra Pattie Maguire
Cilissa Aoibhéann McCann

Dublin Movement and Intimacy Director Sue Mythen
Dublin Casting Director Sarah Jones

For Dermot and the children

Characters

Clytemnestra
wife of Agamemnon

Agamemnon
the Lion of Argos

Cassandra
daughter of Priam and Hecuba

Aegisthus
cousin of Agamemnon

Cilissa
servingwoman of Clytemnestra

Tyndareus
father of Clytemnestra

Setting

Fluid. Sky. Sea. Stars. Wind. Stone. Bronze. Aegean Light.

GIRL ON AN ALTAR

Act One

Music. Sound of the sea. The sky black, studded with stars, let some fall.

Clytemnestra We arrive at night on Aulis' rocky shore. Iphigenia's face streaked with dirt and tears. She doesn't want to be a bride and has fought with me the whole journey. I tell her she will not be just any bride, but the bride of Achilles, the greatest king after her father and some whisper greater. She's having none of it. She wants to go home, play with her pet lamb, her dolls, the other children who have grown up alongside her behind the palace walls of our high green kingdom. I tell her, her father wishes it, that it's only a formality, that after the ceremony I'll take her home till she is fifteen, the proper age for a girl to be married. Agamemnon better allow this. I'm raging with him that he would use his daughter to cement an alliance with these warring savages. And when we arrive he greets me sombrely, his mood strange. He carries his sleeping daughter to her tent. Leave her, he says to the women.

Agamemnon Let her sleep. You can wash her in the morning.

Clytemnestra There's a new scar on his neck, a wound under his left eye, the fist swollen, knuckles vanishing under a darkening bruise.
All is not well?

Agamemnon You've no idea.

Clytemnestra I have to see to the babies, settle them. Why you had to drag us here. Is this another coup? Is that why you made us all come?

Agamemnon Let's not speak of it in front of the child. Settle the twins then join me in my tent.

Clytemnestra And he nods for twenty of his men to accompany me, his royal guard. Twenty. This is serious. He leaves another twenty surrounding Iphigenia's tent. The rest follow him to his floating compound on the cliff. I tend to the babies, leave Cilissa in charge and make my way to the inner sanctum where I find him poring over his maps. He has stripped to the waist, another new wound snaking down his back.

Someone came at you from behind.

Agamemnon While I was exercising Aetha.

Clytemnestra Cowards.

Agamemnon You've nothing to fear. Your life is safe. The war council have agreed a treaty. We're all bound to the peace now.

Clytemnestra You and your treaties. That wound needs dressing and that cut under your eye is infected, needs to be lanced. This is insane. The war hasn't even started and already you're a walking ruin. What bastard went for your face and I'll chop his spine off with my Lydian axe.

And who went for your back?

Whoever it was they meant to take you out. Who was it?

Agamemnon Your gold vest saved me.

Clytemnestra It won't save you forever. I need a bath. I'm covered in welter from the road.

And after I've dipped myself in his silver bath, I find him looking at the sky, the waves breaking on the stony shore below, his black ships rocking in their chains further out, voices in the dark, fires lit, someone plucking a lyre far away, the smell of roasting meat curling up on the wind. A sinister night. Evil and edge in the air.

What are they celebrating?

Agamemnon There's to be a sacrifice tomorrow.

Clytemnestra For Iphigenia's wedding? She's too young to be married. This Achilles, is he groom material? What's he like?

Agamemnon An arrogant warring punk who swings both ways, that's what he's like. Thinks he should be king. Has the whole place in uproar.

Clytemnestra A younger version of you then, bar the swinging.

Agamemnon I think I always put my people first, what's best for the tribe, the kingdom. Not this peacock. Claims his mother was a goddess. Well if she was, amn't I descended from Helios himself? No better lineage than that if he wants to bring the gods into it.

Clytemnestra You're clay like the rest of us. Dust. One generation and we're forgotten.

Agamemnon Don't I know it.

Clytemnestra I'm not happy about this wedding.

Agamemnon It's out of your hands, out of all our hands, the priests have spoken.

Clytemnestra To hell with the priests. Iphigenia has just turned ten. I'm taking her home after the ceremony. She's a small girl. I don't trust them to leave her alone. She's not ready for any of this.

Agamemnon Look, they've rigged the Oracle. An attempt to bring me to heel. If we don't give them Iphigenia there'll be a bloodbath here tomorrow. They'll depose me, slaughter us all, make Achilles their new king.

Clytemnestra You've brought us into a trap. The babies?

Agamemnon The babies too. All of us.

Clytemnestra (*looks at him*) What?

Agamemnon Leave me. Leave me now.

Clytemnestra What is it? What have they done to you? There's something you're not saying.

Agamemnon Go to bed, woman, come, I'll escort you.

Clytemnestra And he walks me to the women's tents, kisses my hand and leaves me there. Very unlike him. I must be losing my charm, still a bit chumpy after the birth of the twins, or he's besotted with one of the camp trollops. It'll pass, always does. Experience has taught me, turn the blind eye, say nothing, no talking to any of them when the war lust is on them. I look in on Iphigenia. She opens her eyes in the glaze of sleep, smiles. Her dressmakers are working quietly beside her, putting the finishing touches to her wedding gown. I leave them to it and go to the babies' tent. Cilissa snoring her head off with a baby in each arm. I lie down beside them. My infant son finds my thumb and clings to it as I sink like a stone into the last innocent sleep I am permitted on this black earth.

SCENE TWO

Dawn. Pink sky. Sound of the sea.

Agamemnon Atarxis, my general, lifts my daughter up to me. She turns to kiss me, a garland of gentians in her shining hair. They have her decked out in white, gold sandals on her small brown feet. I give her the reins and she whoops with delight at the speed of Aetha. And I'm thinking, I can't do this. I cannot do this. The whole camp is armed. Everyone's dander up, Achilles preening in his glittering armour. His eyes flick to my daughter, then back to me, I can hear him thinking, he's calling our bluff, he'll never go through with it. Won't I, you mortal upstart? Won't I indeed? I'll show you what the king of kings is made of. I'll show you what must be given away. I'm the one leading this army to Troy's pink walls if I have to kill you all to do it. Zeus Agamemnon to you, you marauding parvenu. Zeus Agamemnon from the house of Pelops. Zeus Atrides Agamemnon, great-grandson of Helios. The sun god's blood runs in my veins. Veins of gold, you treacherous blue-blood runt.

Clytemnestra I'm shaken out of sleep, Cilissa hissing in my face.

Cilissa They've taken her and beyond in the kitchens they're putting it around that there's to be no wedding but some unspeakable offering on the altar below at the shore.

Clytemnestra Taken who?

Cilissa Iphigenia. She went by on her father's horse at dawn.

Clytemnestra She's with her father. She's safe.

Cilissa The sacrificial fires are lit, priests dancing across the sand with their drums, she's standing on the altar, her dress in tatters.

Clytemnestra What are you saying? Where are the babies?

Cilissa Come, come now!

Clytemnestra Stop your ranting, woman!

Cilissa No listen! The Oracle, the gods, Artemis slighted, Zeus angry, the wind all wrong, Troy a vanishing dream. Iphigenia! They want her.

Clytemnestra Want her for what?

Cilissa She's the sacrifice!
    She leaps over me and is out the flap, tearing along the cliff screaming like a banshee. I tear after her, our feet in ribbons as we pound the shale, haul ourselves down the slope, all the women suddenly behind us and we're roaring, shoving, tripping, sliding down the dunes as she flies ahead in her nightdress.

Clytemnestra The beach thick with all the tribes, armour gleaming, hands on the hilts of their swords, the sky blackening, a glut around the altar, three massive boulders, the men parting like wind in barley as we scythe through them and then . . . oh . . .

Cilissa He's standing on the altar, mask on, obsidian knife in his hand, Iphigenia raised to the skies in his right arm . . .

Clytemnestra Blood on the stones . . . his arms . . . her throat . . .

Cilissa She takes a flying leap at the altar, manages to scale the jagged stone, fury propelling her, wrestles the child from Agamemnon with such force he falls backwards, as she rains kisses like blows on the dying child, trying to shake the life back into her, stanch the river of blood flowing from her neck over her arms, her face, in her mouth, clinging to the girl they've stripped to the waist, and the high priest steps forward, pounding his drum, berating her in his high falsetto, shame on you woman, botching the god's sacrifice, shame on you.

Clytemnestra Shame on me? You have stolen my child, butchered her like a beast of the field! Shame on me? Shame on you, you band of prancing gorillas! May you never reach Troy and if by some trick of fate you do, may you never return, may you die there, howling, a banquet for the crow, the rat, the wild dog, no one to mourn you, none to speak your memory except with hate and scorn, your own mothers cursing you, you savage guests of Time.

Cilissa Her voice low, lethal, the men shifting, coughing, eyes full of fear. Do they actually expect a blessing for this carnage?

Clytemnestra Iphigenia dying in my arms, black clouds rolling across the silver sea, wind rising, rain spattering and then the heavens opening. Iphigenia bucking, choking.

Agamemnon on his knees struggling to get his mask off, her necklace in his hand.

Agamemnon Go! Take her with you before I have to do it all over again. Go before I have to slit your throat too. She flies off the altar, never letting the child from her grip, her women close in as they move through the men who shove and stumble to back out of her way, afraid of her and the procession of keening women. Achilles looks at me, the guarded eyes that still won't give quarter but he knows who's king round here now. There'll be no more trouble, no swaggering wide boys scheming for my throne. He watches as the elite come, bow, kiss my feet, all the tribes with their trumped-up little under-kings. I accept the tributes, the honeyed lies, the deference, without taking my eyes off him. He's the last to come forward. Of course he is. And only because he can't do otherwise, everyone watching, waiting, can see him calculating, can he still swing it his way? The fury he can't contain, prancing, tossing the hair. But he comes finally, kneels like the rest of them, kisses my bloodstained feet, spits out the hollow words. Zeus Agamemnon. That's right, I say as I grip his hand and raise him in the accustomed manner. That's right and don't you forget it. And he snorts and swaggers off, nostrils flaring and I know I'm no god incarnate but I'm the closest he'll ever come to one. Old Colchis comes forward with his sagging diddies, offering me the cup of sacrificial blood to drink, my daughter's blood. I knock it from his hand and grab him by the throat. Atarxis is there in a flash separating us, the whole camp gasping. Cool it, Atarxis says. No more oracles, I say, No more of your Pythian riddles that can be read a thousand ways, you demented old woman. I only read the signs, Colchis mumbles, the sick eyes leaking down the ravines of his face. And what do the signs say now? What do your gods say? What's the gossip from Delphi, and it better be good. The wind, he whines. What about the wind? It's here, he drawls. The wind, I say, the wind was here yesterday, the wind is here today and the wind'll be here tomorrow but my daughter will never be here again. Sing that on your fuckin' altar. To the ships, I shout, raising my sword, slapping on the golden mask. The Oracle has spoken. Our sacrifice has been accepted and deemed fitting. Look at this rain! Hear the wind rising! The signs are for victory. The men roar in relief. They love this sort of crap so I milk it, do the Bacchic dance, sing myself hoarse, stomp and hoof and snort like a stallion as the men go wild and weep and fall to their knees. Zeus Agamemnon, they scream, beating their fists in the air, on their chests, tearing at their hair like a bunch of auld ones at a funeral. In the distance, along the cliff, I see the lonely procession, my wife, my dead child, making their way to the women's tents and I don't know how I'll ever make it right with her again. To the ships, I say, and the exodus for Troy finally begins.

Music. Lights.

Act Two

Ten years later.
   Mycenae. The hilltop. Landscape of amber and green.
Blazing blue sky. Shimmering heat.

Clytemnestra Thunder of the hooves as he comes galloping
through the cypress trees, leaps off Aetha, kisses the earth,
flinging fistfuls of it in the air, the bull neck thrown back as
he releases a sound somewhere between a wail and his big
mad laugh, holding out his jewelled fingers for all to kiss as
they fall on their knees, weeping, roaring, my lord, my lord,
king of kings, you're safe, you're home, you won again, beat
the sly Trojans into their fat pink dirt, blood pouring down
the walls of their smoking city, churning through their ruined
land for decades to come. And he smiles, looking at me
coolly from under the fringe of his sea-matted, salt-tangled
hair. And for a second I see him as they do and time flies
backward and the heart lurches in this rancorous breast, the
big bruised fact of him, the scars on his arms of bronze, the
doomed eyes in that wild arrogant face, the huge Mycenaean
nose sniffing the air, the olives, the vines, the sun beating for
him alone as he shimmers and stalks and works the crowd,
his prostrate people shrieking, laughing, shoving, to get a
hold of the sacred hand that skims over them in benediction.
He goes to the war widows, a coven of weeping witches,
makes a fuss of them, whispering sweet nothings about the
bravery of their dead husbands who fell on the beaches, in
the hills, up and down the valleys, on the pink ramparts of
that fabled city, how bravely they fought, how well they died,
their bereft women will be taken care of, for sure they will,
honoured and feted as the wives of heroes and valiant braves.
All the time his predator's eye roving over the good lookers,

clocking, storing up for an idle night of kiss and tell when he might have need of them for an hour or so of sweet remembrance. And he lets them paw and kiss and stroke his war-ravaged, sea-wracked carcass, legs wide apart like a statue of himself, like the first sea god dripping from the waves, trident in his hand, eyes the colour of the Aegean itself. And then he strides towards me, taking the palace steps in threes and he has me by the hand.

Agamemnon Time has been to work on her and sorrow too, the eyes inscrutable with subterfuge. How much do I know, I can hear her thinking. I know it all, my love. I know it all. I know that little girl who stands behind you clinging to Cilissa's skirt is the little bastard you were busy making while I was away. I know who her father is. My cousin Aegisthus. Looking at me in consternation through the battered vestiges of his pride, murderous smirk on his puss. Never thought to see me again swanking from the plains of Troy. Coward. Lump of incest. Child of child eaters, madness and revenge whirling in his wolf shark veins. Woman, I say, as I kiss her for the crowd, woman, where's your taste? She pulls away, raising her voice, not for me, for the watching tribe.

Clytemnestra Welcome home, my lord. Ten years is a long time to wait for anyone.

Agamemnon Patience was never one of your virtues.
    Faithless wagon. Charlatan to your fingertips. Liar to the core.
    But still, the sight of her, the smell of her, the waist on her, the old flame ignites once I'm in front of her, the body curving under the flowing dress down to her jewelled toes, the clasp in her hair, the diamonds slinking along her throat, a gift from me, a summer's morning in the long ago, our first infant in the cradle. Iphigenia.
    Unforgiving witch. You wear them today of all days when you have caskets to choose from. These you put on

24

for my triumphant return. These to remind me, as if I need reminding.

I kiss her again as the crowd cheers and Aegisthus stares. She gasps, struggles, the old magic doing what the old magic does. Cilissa laughs outright and then bows her head, her body rocking.

Cilissa, I'm glad I amuse you and it's well you're looking, God bless you.

Cilissa (*kneels; kisses his hand*) God bless you too, my lord.

He looks at me closely to read what's in my face, to see if I hate him too. What I've seen in this house down the decades is beyond hate. Aegisthus fumes, hand on his sword as the crowd watch. Are we going to have another bloodbath at the palace door?

Agamemnon Cassandra, I call and the little prophetess stands out from my entourage. Clytemnestra's eyes narrow, the cheeks reddening as she sizes up this beauty half her age.

You parade your lover. Watch me parade mine. Two can play this silly game.

Clytemnestra Oh another shining tart, another little piece of war booty.

Agamemnon This is Priam's daughter, the prophetess who sang of our victory as we shivered and starved on the beaches among the rats and the shale. This is Cassandra.

Clytemnestra She's young. So young. Far from home. Her father, mother, siblings gone. Mowed down by you. What must go through her mind when you're on top of her?

Cassandra Stone lions everywhere. His emblems. His ego. Fountains gushing silver water, the burnt hills, olive branches crippled with fruit, the smell of horses, all his people, hard weathered faces, the war widows in black, a flock of demented crows, the children lined up behind her, his queen, Clytemnestra, their heads bowed, in their best clothes which aren't much. My mother was right. These people are savages. They only look good on a battlefield running into the arms of a blade. What they're bred for, it seems. Not for them the hours of pointless ease. Smoke, blood, flames, these the things they crave.

Aegisthus Smitten. She's smitten again. Knew if she clapped eyes on him. There she stands, batting the eyelashes, smiling falsely. She can't help herself, eyes pouring lust, jealous of this Trojan waif he holds by the wrist. Cousin, he says, turning on me that hooded eagle stare, lips tight with rage he cannot spill in front of the tribe. If we were in a dark hallway we'd go at it with knives.

Agamemnon Go home, cousin, before I mow you down here in front of them.

Aegisthus He eyes my daughter. Instinct picking her out from his own children. Child killer. Like his father. Old Atreus carved up my brothers, toddling infants, put them in the casserole and served them up to my father. I stand my ground.

Cousin, you'll find there's been a few changes in your long absence. You'll find your wife has all of Sparta behind her. And neither am I without allies. I'd tread carefully if I was you.

Agamemnon Still scuttling and scheming for my throne, Aegisthus? The old quarrel. The old gripe. Still whingeing I've stolen your birthright?

Aegisthus Like your father stole my father's.

Agamemnon (*grabs him; forces him to kneel*) My father was the stronger man, the fitter king until you ran a sword through him as he kneeled at his prayers. The blood in you is mad, coursing down the generations, a slime over everything. Your own sister your mother? Perverse. Disgusting. The thought of you anywhere near my wife. I could kill you right now. Go back to where you came from, take your band of wide boys with you and let me not clap eyes on you again in this world or the next one.

Aegisthus His men poised, advancing nonchalantly, swaggering, lean, lethal from a decade of carnage. I look to Clytemnestra for the signal. There is none. She looks away.

Clytemnestra Aegisthus' and his men disappear out the east gate. Mine stand there waiting. An hour ago I had their loyalty but that was before he stood in front of them. Their eyes aflame with wonder, the enchanted air that always seems to surround him, though some of them too young to have known him, boys with wooden swords when he left for the dream of Troy. But they've heard the stories, the legends, he's in their blood. I'm tempted to rally them, release the curdling battle cry and see him hacked to pieces in front of my eyes. But they'll never harm him and neither will I. Impossible.

Agamemnon She calls the children to come forward.

Clytemnestra The ones that are left.

Cassandra Orestes, he says, a question in his eyes. And he lifts the boy off the ground and with his other arm he scoops up the girl and kisses them both lavishly.

Clytemnestra His eyes rest on Leda who stands behind me.

Agamemnon And who have we here?

Clytemnestra This is Leda, my daughter Leda.

Agamemnon Your daughter Leda?

Clytemnestra Yes, my daughter Leda. He places a hand on her bowed head and looks at me.

Agamemnon I took one from you so I owe you this one in return.

Clytemnestra A swap is it? Am I meant to be grateful you don't put her out on the mountain for the jackals to dine on? Am I meant to forget? Do you actually think you have the right to forgive me anything? I'm speechless.

Agamemnon That's it. Leave it all unspoken.

Clytemnestra Iphigenia.

Agamemnon I'm offering you a clean slate. We start with today. We leave yesterday where it belongs. Come, Cassandra.

Clytemnestra He walks through the ebony door calling the children to follow him, Cassandra on his arm. Leda hangs back, holding on to my dress. Go, I say, go with them, he has called you, and she runs on her skinny legs to catch up. He turns to wait for her and they go within, his armed guard, weapons clanging, shadow him.

SCENE TWO

Inside. A fountain. A lone voice sings.

Cassandra I'm put in the harem among the neglected hard-eyed women who wander the gated halls, their young daughters by the hand. They sit around the fountains plaiting their hair and fighting. They sleep all day and play dice or cards all night. They drink their heads off. They look at me suspiciously. They'd like to do me wrong. I ignore them. They're not my destiny. The old ones lie in their hammocks looking into the nowhere, having spent their whole lives here, the old king's once-upon-a-time paramours or forgotten daughters of the house born the wrong side of the sheets. Birds fly over, starlings, cranes, swans. Before dawn it is usual to hear muffled weeping, the lonely wail as another of them gives up the ghost. Then one of his soldiers comes and the women hiss and whisper and look at me desperately as I'm led away and the gates are locked again.

Clytemnestra He's in the map room. Parchments of skies, seas, the known lands, stretched across the walls, the tables, the floor. He drinks a cup of wine, casements open to catch the breeze, a rug laid on the terrace heaped with food. I stand there until he deigns to speak. We've kept a wide berth since he's come home. From what I can gather he's been sleeping alone. And he has been careful about Leda, has sent her gifts and insured she is given the same honour and respect in the household as Orestes and Electra. I can't fault him on that. And my own apartments are full to bursting with the plunder of Ilion. Diamonds, sapphires, pearls, ropes of rubies, crates of gold, gowns from the dead Trojan queen's wardrobes. All hers by right. All Hecuba's stuff.

Agamemnon Ah.
(*Takes her hand.*)
Come, let's eat, they can do without us in hall this evening.

Clytemnestra Never thought I'd sit on a rug with you again.

Agamemnon What did you think?

Clytemnestra That you'd die there.

Agamemnon You wished it?

Clytemnestra No I didn't wish it.

Agamemnon You did and you wish it still. I wished it too.

Clytemnestra I thought you wouldn't dare come home.

Agamemnon Well, here I am, at your service again.

Clytemnestra And he laughs and for a second he's the boy I fell for in the long ago. He had few scars then, not like now, stretched across the rug, grooved and welted and lined like one of his sea maps.
    You've a few new trophies on your pelt.

Agamemnon Goes with the territory.

Clytemnestra I have to marvel at the endurance of the man, all the blows he has taken.

Agamemnon And your scars?

Clytemnestra My scars?

Agamemnon Is there anything I can do?

Clytemnestra I doubt even the great Atrides Agamemnon can bring back the dead.

Agamemnon I'll give you more daughters, you're young enough.

Clytemnestra We've been allotted our portion for this time round.

Agamemnon Then what am I to do with you? If we can't live as man and wife. Are you asking me to put you aside?

Clytemnestra You took my daughter, your daughter . . . I carried her dying from that altar. And you ask me what you're supposed to do with me? You ask me if you should put me aside?

Agamemnon My hands were tied.

Clytemnestra Iphigenia's hands were tied.

Agamemnon They would've taken us all out.

Clytemnestra Better if they had.

Agamemnon Don't say that.

Clytemnestra You're right. We don't deserve to die, to rest, we don't deserve anything anymore.

Agamemnon She sits with her head bowed, this capable woman who has kept the kingdom in order my long years away. I chose well, the wife I needed in the end, though there is much about her that is hard to stomach. Aegisthus, I say.

Clytemnestra What about him?

Agamemnon Another man would have you killed. But I understand. You did it to wound me.

Clytemnestra Did I? Did it?

Agamemnon What do you think? It has certainly wounded you. In your own eyes and in the eyes of the tribe. They don't like you. It was a stupid move and one not worthy of you. You know I'm right on this. A queen should be untouchable, above reproof. You've given them leverage and that was stupid, now they can whisper about you in the dark.

Clytemnestra And they don't whisper in the dark about you?

Agamemnon What's to whisper? Everything I did was for them, for the tribe. They know this and they love me. They worship me.

Clytemnestra They're fools, still reading bones and entrails, still trying to augur the flight of birds, conjure the wind, parse the sea, still waiting for the gods to come down and walk among them. They'll wait. The gods are gone and why wouldn't they be?

Agamemnon Officially they're still here, you're looking at one.

Clytemnestra So now you're a god?

Agamemnon What's a god but a man magnified? No, I'm no god, I'm flesh and bone, but I'm a king and your anointed husband and you betrayed me with my cousin. I don't forgive that. I'll never forgive that. I should put you in the harem, let the foot soldiers use you, rot there under them.

Clytemnestra You're no king. You're a tainted cut throat, a daughter slayer.

Agamemnon I have gone, soft as a woman, pussyfooting round you. I've honoured your little bastard with Aegisthus, I've showered you with the riches of Troy, I have bent over backwards to please you. It was ten years ago.

They sprung it on me. I was surrounded. It was a vicious power struggle, that little skunk Achilles wrangling for my throne and the over-kingship. If it was now I'd have gone a lamb to the slaughter before they'd touch a hair on her head. I know that now. I didn't then, my blood was up, Hercules singing in my veins, egging me on. Can't you see how it was for me? You have no right to judge me on this matter. I can do that well enough myself.

Clytemnestra You haven't gone to her grave.

Agamemnon Nor will I. I won't find her there.

Clytemnestra Guilt won't let you. Your boundless pride won't let you.

Agamemnon Neither of those. I just can't bear to.

Clytemnestra You want to pretend it never happened?

Agamemnon Is there another way?

Clytemnestra Your father, Old Atreus, the same, carving up his infant nephews. Your little cousins? Aegisthus' brothers? I heard this story as a child, whispered by the nursery slaves. And I thought then as I think now, this is an old fragment from some barbaric age. People don't behave like that in these enlightened times. You put our daughter on an altar for the wind to change. And you sit here sipping your wine as if it happened to someone else. As if it has nothing to do with you or me.

Agamemnon Then tell me what to do. Tell me what will make it right between us again.

She doesn't answer, bows slowly, mockingly, walks from the room.

Clytemnestra I go to the children's quarters. Cilissa is settling them for the night. The girls pull me to them, their faces hot and the sweet child breath in my hair. They never want me to leave. I go to Orestes' chamber, he is sitting up in bed waiting for me. Next spring he'll be in the training grounds, this lovely gentle boy, living among men, I'll hardly see him. Pappi is taking me hunting at dawn, he says, we're going to get a stag. Then you better get to sleep, I say and he kisses me and I cover him and sit by him until Cilissa comes to sing her lullabies. I meet the Trojan girl, Cassandra, as I cross the inner courtyard. I watch as she is led to the passageway that gives on to his rooms. My women undress me, wrap me in my night sheet. I crawl into bed, my ghost child beside me. I dread the nights because she comes to torture me with her eyes of muck and the blood spilling from the gash to her throat as if it was cut a second ago. And her fury, you'd think it would split the walls as she howls out the injustice, that I am still here and will not come to her though she has begged me, that she will wait no longer, that she will come to me. And I believe none of these things and still they happen.

SCENE THREE

Mycenae. Interior.

Cassandra I'm given my own chamber in a side wing off his, slave girls to wait on me. I dine in the great hall, seated beside him, his queen the other side. She never looks at me. He sends for me most nights and clings to me like one of the damned, swathes of sorrow coming off him. No hint now of the bragging, swaggering barbarian that put the heart crossways in the bravest of them back home. The Lion of Argos they called him. He lies frozen, eyes fixed on the ceiling, an oak felled by forked lightening. His children romp around the fountains below my window or run through the halls, gay, shrieking, oblivious. And all the time I'm waiting for her, his queen, to pounce, to do the proud deed. And I want to say to her when she passes me with her nose in the air. Get on with it, woman. Get it over with. Stop torturing him. Take away this uncertainty because who would've thought, but I begin to hope. In this wild land where every goatherd is a trumped-up king. I begin to hope because the visions are gone. No more blinding tableaus and haunted voices that leave me shaking with their import. And I'm carrying a child, his child, and my only wish is to see it born. Safe. Healthy. Here. I'm learning what it is to live in the now. The curse has lifted. I can't see her axe descending or his silver bath or the prophecy foretold. And I miss their certainty even as I bask in the ordinary. A slave girl now. But in the small hours, between moon and sun, the evil dark, he sometimes says, what do you see, stranger? What do you see in store for me? And I answer him in his language, only what a fool can see, what anyone with a fligget of sense can see, terror, horror, suffering. And he laughs and takes my hand. Sleep, I say, I'll watch for you till light. And he closes his eyes with relief. I mean something to him that I shouldn't while it is her he craves.

Agamemnon I hold my patience. Give her time. All flowers in time bend towards the sun. She's had too much freedom. My long absence, has got used to doing things her way, not having to consider the mere wishes of a man. She needs the yoke again but I won't force it yet. I do what I can to soften her, visit Iphigenia's grave, prostrate myself there, naked like a criminal, have the priests flog me till I'm a seething pulp, have them dig up her bones, bury the girl again, have a statue of her likeness erected in gold, call in the shower from Delphi to strut their stuff. They lay it on, prancing the altar, incense burning our eyes, the hollow songs as they call down the immortals. I believe none of it. I didn't then and I don't now. The girl is gone. Clytemnestra watches it all, unmoved, face of marble, eyes untranslatable.

Clytemnestra He turns to me in hall one evening, wine on him, sentimental. There is nothing I would not do to have your good opinion again, he says.

Agamemnon She looks at me a minute, a flicker of yielding there, but then she thinks better of it and looks away as if I haven't spoken.

34

Clytemnestra The Trojan girl is pregnant, his paramour, the one he calls the little prophetess. And if he isn't flaunting her, he's not hiding her away either. The girl seems to move through her own separate air though she bows every time we pass and never sits before me at table and gives me all my dues. I can't fault her but neither can I bring myself to speak to her. I send the midwives to examine her. I will not be accused of neglect though the gall rises. Aegisthus sends tributes and messages, begging for forgiveness, for leave to present himself, but Agamemnon refuses to see him. This I'm glad of, it was never a love match and now I've no use for him.

Cilissa It gets more difficult to hide the discord between them. They put on a good face in public but in private they grieve and seethe. I find her on the floor one evening, face in the rushes. Another evening she's in the outer chamber, all bedecked in the spoils of Troy. Is this what he wants, she says, strutting the halls in a dead woman's trinkets as if none of it ever happened? She won't eat, won't wash, can't sleep. She's frightening the children, stares at them as if they're strangers and they come running to me crying. She sits at high table, a statue, one of those broken sculptures from the ruined palaces of the golden age, lips trembling, spilling her wine and not noticing. And Agamemnon, he looks at her desperately, the Trojan captive always by his side as if he cannot breathe without her, as if only she can protect him from whatever he sees in his doomed inward eye. My lady, I say, we must bathe you. She looks at me with her ravaged face, the horror in it as if we've just lifted Iphigenia from the altar, carrying her along Aulis' rocky shore, the little girl still choking. Between them they couldn't even finish it. The priests. Him. All the warring tribes, the raging wind, the flying rain.

Clytemnestra What?

Cilissa You're not fit to be seen.

Clytemnestra Ah Cilissa, let me be.

Cilissa What is it, my lady? What is it that ails you so?

Clytemnestra My mother went mad too, Cilissa, and I'm her daughter.

Cilissa, always there. Her mother was my wet nurse, fed us both from the one gorging breast. A captured Amazon. And Cilissa for all her years in harness has that Amazon forest free way about her.

What ails me is the terrible thing I cannot bring myself to do.

Cilissa What terrible thing?

Clytemnestra Put myself in the grave on top of her.

Cilissa Don't be talking nonsense. Let these things pass, let the dead child go, we've all buried children. What's so different about your grief? So elevated? So proud? You wear it like a crown.

Clytemnestra Her little neck. Like an animal. Held down. Howling in the rain. Surely if there's rhyme or reason, the old laws, a daughter can't be snatched and butchered on a tribal whim.

Cilissa You're talking to a slave. I've lived from the cradle on the whims of my betters.

Clytemnestra I gave you your freedom when I came into my portion.

Cilissa We're never free just because another wishes it on us. Dust yourself down, girl, go back to your husband, make more children while you can, bend the knee, forget, that's all he wants.

Clytemnestra I can't.

Cilissa Pretend. You don't have to love him.

Clytemnestra But I do, Cilissa. I do love him.

Cilissa And it mortifies you because of Iphigenia? You think if you go back to him you're betraying her? You're not. My mother always said the gods fit the burden to the back. Agamemnon's not a cruel man. It's not his true nature is what I mean.

Clytemnestra They sacrificed another girl before they left Troy.

Cilissa I heard.

Clytemnestra One of Hecuba's daughters. They say Hecuba was there. And you know who ordered the sacrifice?

Cilissa I do.

Clytemnestra And who performed it?

Cilissa I do.

Clytemnestra It's becoming a habit. Soon it'll be normal and before you can turn round it'll be a law. Before it was ring giving, ring taking, ships of gold and ships of spices, poets and harpists in the banquet hall. And if a sacrifice was wanted it was a calf or a deer. Now it's girls. The blood of spotless girls these new gods want. What is this terrible new pact among men? I no longer know this man they call Zeus Atrides Agamemnon.

SCENE FOUR

Mycenae. Interior. A bed. A casement open wide. Stars.

Cassandra Grey wet days, the passages draughty, leaves whirling round the rooms, days of iron, days of metal. Agamemnon rarely sends for me now. He kisses my hand if he comes across me. Little prophetess, he says, do you have everything you need. Twins. I'm having twins. Since the voices have gone, I have no idea who I am, begin to forget I am the daughter of a king. I'm just another slave girl who goes in fear of her life, in fear of everything.

37

Clytemnestra He comes to my chamber in the small hours. Wine on him, pulls me to him, kisses me.

What are you doing?

Agamemnon What do you think I'm doing, woman, breaking horses?

Clytemnestra We have to, he says, we have to, silencing my protests with his mouth. Now my love, he says, the stars are there . . .

Agamemnon The stars are there and we are here and I'm going to give you another girl. An incomparable girl. I'm going to give you another Iphigenia.

Clytemnestra That you'll never do.

Agamemnon No, listen . . .

Clytemnestra No, don't speak about her, don't call her up. Don't mention her name.

Agamemnon Okay, I won't, I won't, I only want to say that there is nothing I wouldn't do for you, nothing.

Clytemnestra My love, he says, I've known you since you were six.

Agamemnon In your ponytail running through your father's house. The first time I saw you. And here we are, here we still are despite it all and the sands of time run fast and the sands of time run free. And she listens and doesn't push me away. And though she'll never be eighteen again, it's easy to worship here. And I wonder why she has such a hold over me. Others I can take or leave, but this one, this one. I see all the Clytemnestras I've ever known, memory after memory laid down. The first fatal bolt from the blue. It lodges here still despite all she has done to cut me from her life.

Clytemnestra I conjure up another Agamemnon. The boy with the visionary eyes, the golden prince of my girlhood who brought me nothing but joy, not this battle-scarred warlord with his daughter's ghost trailing him. I look at his hands and cannot believe what these hands have done.

Agamemnon Celestial woman.

Clytemnestra Man of clay.

Agamemnon Is this not lovely?

Clytemnestra You have never not been lovely, I almost answer. It isn't true, but when did lovers ever speak a word of truth.
 Lovelier than the little prophetess?

Agamemnon Leave the little prophetess out of it, only a girl, a lonely girl far from home. What would you have me do with her?

Clytemnestra Send her back to where she came from.

Agamemnon After she's brought to childbed.

Clytemnestra Okay. After.

Agamemnon And Aegisthus?

Clytemnestra You've no right to ask me about Aegisthus. You ran. Afraid to face me.

Agamemnon I didn't run. I've never run from anything least of all a contrary woman. I was fighting for my life, bringing a band of murderous savages to heel.

Clytemnestra I don't want to hear it.

Agamemnon And I don't want to hear your excuses for taking my cousin into my bed.

Clytemnestra What excuses? I've never excused him. Why should I? I owe you nothing.

Agamemnon You owe me everything. I'm your husband.

Clytemnestra Aegisthus was my husband.

Agamemnon He was never your husband!

Clytemnestra He deserves the title more than you. It was he put me back together after your wonderful husbandry. It was he kept me alive. Aegisthus. Not you. Aegisthus. The children. Leda was born. I thought having Leda might take the, the . . . You danced on that altar.

Agamemnon You think I wanted to dance?

Clytemnestra I saw you.

Agamemnon You saw what you wanted to see. I'm the king, the king has to play many roles.

Clytemnestra You danced on your daughter's blood.

Agamemnon A body can dance while the mind does another thing.

Clytemnestra You'd never have agreed to put Orestes on that altar.

Agamemnon They didn't demand it.

Clytemnestra You'd never have agreed. But a girl. You can do anything to a girl.

Agamemnon What happened at Aulis is none of your concern. The affairs of men, no place for you in them.

Clytemnestra Get out! Just get out!

Agamemnon Stop! Stop! Stop right now. Don't say one more thing you can't take back because I've been more than patient with you.

Clytemnestra The affairs of men! Get out! Fling me from the window! Hang me in chains like your mother! I'm dead already! I'm with the dead.

Agamemnon You're losing the run of yourself, you're moving somewhere beyond men and women. I won't follow you.

Clytemnestra Just say you were wrong. Say it. Say she was never here, say I dreamt it all, say there was never a girl called Iphigenia.

Agamemnon I was made. You were there. You saw. Did you have to drag her kicking and screaming? Hold her down? Slide the knife?

Clytemnestra Say it. You killed her.

Agamemnon Okay. I killed her.

Clytemnestra Your own blood.

Agamemnon My own blood.

Clytemnestra Your daughter.

Agamemnon My daughter.

Clytemnestra And wasn't it beautiful?

Agamemnon What?

Clytemnestra I saw your face. Was it a new feeling? A first?

Agamemnon Stop this now.

Clytemnestra I try to understand. What was it? You and the gods battling it out on the altar? Zeus Atrides Agamemnon and his gods?

Agamemnon It was about men. Men! I was losing control of the army. You know this. They thought I'd never do it.

Clytemnestra But you showed them! You showed them what Zeus Agamemnon is made of?

Agamemnon Yes I showed them.

Clytemnestra The king.

Agamemnon The king of kings.

Clytemnestra The king of kings. Do you see her? Does she come to you?

Agamemnon No she doesn't come to me.

Clytemnestra You don't miss her? You didn't have a soft spot for her? She certainly had for you.

Agamemnon If I say I miss her, you'll say I have no right to miss her.

Clytemnestra You have no right to miss her!

Agamemnon I know I have no right to miss her! I live with that. I live with it every day but easy fantasise safe in our beds how we'd go to the ends of the earth for the ones we love. Different story with the knife to your throat. You or her? You'd do the same.

Clytemnestra No I wouldn't.

Agamemnon You've never been tested the way I've been tested.

Clytemnestra You could've gone to Troy without leading all the tribes. You could've gone as just another marauding savage.

Agamemnon So that's what I am, a marauding savage?

Clytemnestra There was never any need to go to Troy. You rule huge territories, you have Crete, you have most of the islands. This land is good, more than sustains us. You didn't have to go to Troy. You didn't have to do it. You didn't have to kill her.

Agamemnon My love . . . there are only things that happen to us, things that happen to us and then we're gone, as shocked as when we came. Let it go. Come back to me. Have some pity on a desperate man. I'm devastated without you.

Clytemnestra And what am I without you? Go. Leave me. I can't abide you near me. Your filthy hands. Your stinking, filthy, daughter-murdering hands.

Agamemnon I put my clothes on as she watches in silence. I pause in the doorway. One last chance for her to call me back. Reverse this madness. She turns her face to the wall. So be it.

Clytemnestra He's lost to me now. I've refused him the one thing he has left to offer. Himself. He won't forgive that. And if I know him, he won't ask again.

Agamemnon In the morning I send six of my men in full armour to escort her to the harem.

Clytemnestra The gates clang shut behind me and then they're locked.

SCENE FIVE

Mycenae. Interior.

Cassandra I'm moved into the queen's apartments. Agamemnon comes in the evening and bids me sing. I'm going to marry you, he says, after your babes are born. I pour his wine as he stares off into nowhere.

Cilissa I meet him in the south passage.

Agamemnon Cilissa.

Cilissa Your queen.

Agamemnon I have no queen.

Cilissa You can't.

Agamemnon I'm going to pretend I didn't hear you say that and if you set any store on your life you will never speak to me of her again. Now get off your knees and go to work.

Cilissa It's unwise to put her away like this, and her with half the kingdom on her side and allies of her father's, the great Tyndareus, stretching way up north.

Agamemnon I'll deal with her allies, don't you worry, Cilissa.

I look at this woman, the great height of her, the Amazon blood fighting with the slave. I've known her since she was a child, used wrestle her in the training grounds of Sparta and she often bested me. But she's Clytemnestra's spy now.

Cilissa May I see her?

Agamemnon You may not. Cut her out, Cilissa. Cut her out of your heart. If I can then so can you.

Cilissa But the children, they're asking for her, they're frightened.

Agamemnon She has no children.

Cilissa A shattered man, desperately trying to hold it together, the hard words from the bitter mouth, she has flayed him to the core. I make one last attempt.

But you have known her so long.

Agamemnon Counts for nothing now. You think I'm hard on her, Cilissa. I'm not. I protected that one, froze and starved on the beaches of Ilion while she sat here by the fire with her lover.

SCENE SIX

The harem.

Clytemnestra The wind howls through the draughty rooms and rattles the harem gates. The women huddle around the braziers to keep warm, the tiles cold under our feet. In all my years at Argos, I never deigned to visit this place. Never gave these lonely neglected women a thought, though I approved the accounts every quarter, so much grain, cloth, wine, kif. But I never cared to see them, to look out for their welfare. Yes, I heard the odd bit of gossip from time to time, General so-and-so has a healthy son from one of the pleasure women, but never a mention of the girl infants. And here they are, a flock of small girls from ebony black to palest white, half feral, with the weak limbs and dull eyes of those confined too long. The old women lie in their hammocks, wrapped in moulting bear skins, ochre smeared on their toothless mouths, kohl streaming down their ravaged faces. And I think, I have allowed this, this place of forgotten souls where time stands still, never to see God's good earth and run in the meadows and splash in the streams and know ordinary mortal love. I have allowed all this. I find a pallet in a remote room with bones piled high in a corner. Sleep comes in fits and starts. I wander the rooms in search of I don't know what and I come across her. Leda. She's lying by the inner gate. Leda, I say, but she doesn't stir. I lift her up. Leda, it's me. I take her with me to the room of bones and she clings to me and weeps, the shocking outraged sobs of the powerless child. I'm afraid she'll choke as I hold on to her skinny torso. Leda, my darling I'm here, I'm here now. This is all because of me. My foolish pride, my rage, my arrogance that is like a man's. Leda, I say, it's okay. No, she says, no, it's not okay, and she wails again.

SCENE SEVEN

Argos. Interior.

Agamemnon Joy and sorrow. Bitter and sweet. It's done. She's gone. Let her rot and die. I have a new love. The little prophetess. The children have stopped asking where their mother is, where Leda has gone. I take them in my arms, my beautiful son, too beautiful for a boy, one of Hyacinthus' kind if I'm not mistaken, and my handsome girl, as if she'd swapped faces with her brother in the womb. When you're older you'll understand, I say, when you're older I will tell you about the ways of men and women who fall out of love. The little prophetess is bursting out of her clothes. Two new babes coming for the House of Atreus, the kingdom in good order, the borders quiet, new sea lanes opening east and west, the coffers full. Clytemnestra could have had all this. And I know I have to finish her off, but each day I delay it. It's bad politics. If anyone gets wind of this, they'll think I'm weak and scheme to strike. I would. But after a cup of wine I call to mind what she was to me in the long ago and I can't bring myself to give the order. And the children? My father killed my mother. I was nine. Watched as she was dragged through these halls and hung over the great fountain, watched her choking until my father gave the signal for the soldiers to pull on her legs to break her neck. His hand on my shoulder, now lad, that's how you sort out a whore, may you never have to do the same.

SCENE EIGHT

Sparta. Interior.

Aegisthus Knew sooner or later the monster in him would gain the upper hand. And Clytemnestra all the time waiting for him. In her sleep calling out his name. When I lay on top of her, knew by some alchemy she had switched us in the dark, was conjuring him up. Well we all do that. Can't hold that against her. But I do. And now he's put her aside and my daughter too. My little Leda. Rumours coming thick and fast, he's slayed her in her bath, he's strung the child up over the bed chamber door, he's locked her in the old palace, in the dark caverns, chained to the wall, a nest of rats and stoats to wait upon her. Well she never loved me, though I lavished on her all the things they say a woman craves. We ride into Tyndareus' fat lands. I send a party ahead through the rolling purlieu with gifts for the old king and a request for five minutes of his time.

Tyndareus Aegisthus comes bowing and scraping, bearing too many gifts. I'm related to him, for my sins, twice removed on the mother's side.

What's your bother, cousin?

Aegisthus No bother, Tyndareus, bar the one bother.

Tyndareus Agamemnon. Yourself and Agamemnon. Sure that's the oldest spat. None of my concern.

Aegisthus Every bit your concern.

If it wasn't for him, Agamemnon would never be sitting on my throne.

Tyndareus I think the latest news may be your concern, he says. Go on.

Aegisthus Your daughter.

Tyndareus Clytemnestra? What about her?

Aegisthus He's thrown her away.

Tyndareus He'd never do that to me.

Aegisthus I'm telling you he has.

Tyndareus He'd never dare do that to me.

Aegisthus Rumour has it he's hung her from one of the cypresses that grow beside Iphigenia's tomb. And my daughter Leda hasn't been seen. I'm in fear of her life. Maybe he's taken her out too.

Tyndareus A child's a child and blood is blood and no one spills blood of mine without he pays dear for it. Tell me, Aegisthus, what do you make of my daughter?

Aegisthus Isn't she a princess of Sparta and don't I revere her and would protect her interests if allowed. If she's still alive.

Tyndareus If indeed.

I look at the ugly runt. The honeyed words. This isn't about Clytemnestra or his child. This is about the balance of power. This is about keeping these cut throats off my lands, all the vicious tribes who keep shifting alliance for gain. He must have a lot of them backing him to dare show his face here. If I come in on Agamemnon's side he doesn't stand a chance. But if I back this pup, they'll all descend scrapping for precedence and position and Agamemnon is gone. They're sick of him, only waiting to find his weak spot. I'm old, too old for this, never want to see another battlefield.

Leave me, Aegisthus, your news disturbs an old man's ease. Rest your bones. I'll give you my decision soon.

And he bows and walks backwards from the room.

SCENE NINE

Mycenae. Interior.

Cassandra The babes come, a boy, a girl. Antenor and Thalassa. I lie in Clytemnestra's bed, her tapestries on the wall, her rugs from Tyre, her enamelled cups from Inxor, her jewels, robes, footstools from Troy. The babies sleep in my arms, tiny puckered faces. Agamemnon kisses my hand, blesses the newborns, holds them naked to the sun, the golden casements wide, murmurs some prayer in a language I do not understand. Where is Clytemnestra, I say, where is your queen? You are my queen, he says. And the voices return, the pictures, the visions and I'm afraid what I see coming down the line.

Cilissa Skirmishes along the borders of the kingdom, Agamemnon is on patrol, parleying and fighting and when I pass him on the stairs or the terraces with his entourage, the cold set face looking through me. I understand. I remind him of her. The children are subdued. They go about their days but a light has gone out of them. And I fear for her. Her name is forbidden. Leda's too. The whispered rumours are frightening but I have it from Atarxis that she is still kept in the harem. I go there, hover around the old palace, the fallen pillars, the faded mosaics and frescoes in the old amber and gold of a vanished time. The gates are well guarded. In the shadowy passages I glimpse figures moving to and fro. The stench carries on the wind like the lair of some sleeping monster. The soldiers tell me to get lost. They see the tattoo on my cheek that marks me for a slave. I stand my ground. I say, I am Clytemnestra's free woman and I have permission to see her. From who? one of them says. From Agamemnon, I say. I have a message for her from the king. Then where is your pass, another says, with his emblem and his seal. Are you questioning our king, I say. I'll go right now and tell him his word counts for nothing with you little skunks. And I turn and march off. It works. They run after me as I reach the broken statue of Artemis, beetles crawling from her eyes. Go in, they say, and give your message, and they bang the gates after me and return to their dicing. I find her in a room of bones. Thigh bones, rib bones, ankle bones, skulls stacked to the vaulted ceiling, wisps of dead hair floating in the dirty gold air. She sits in a corner, the child in her arms.

Clytemnestra Ah Cilissa, I knew you wouldn't let me down.

Cilissa And Leda. She's cold.

Clytemnestra You're too late. She's gone. I tried to get food for her but they fight over scraps and at night the wolf women come.

Cilissa What wolf women?

Clytemnestra They want Leda. They eat their dead.

Cilissa I take the child, a little dress of bones, the lips brown as mud, the teeth bared. I wrap her in my shawl.

Clytemnestra Orestes? Electra?

Cilissa They're well, Orestes has gone to the boys' barracks.

Clytemnestra And Electra?

Cilissa Electra goes around with me. I sleep beside her bed.
I lay out some bread, figs, olives, a goblet from her own
private table. I pour some wine. I have to feed her slowly and
then I lead her to the fountain and wash her as best
I can. Women gather and stare. I hiss and click my tongue
and they back off. I take my lady back to her room of bones,
she seems safest here. I gather up the dead child.
I say, you're alive, my lady, and that's something. I'll find a
way to see you again, though I don't know how. I walk
through the painted harridans, the old scarecrows, the dirty
naked children with matted hair and eyes of desperation. My
mother died in a place like this when she was sold into
Thebes after the house of Tyndareus had no more use for her.
Apparently she was an oddity, her one breast considered an
aphrodisiac for those perverts from the swamps. I bang on
the rusty bronze for the soldiers to let me through. They
want to examine my bundle. I uncover the child's rotting
face. Leda, I say, the little princess of Argos, Aegisthus' much
loved daughter, the great Tyndareus' granddaughter and if
you don't let me bury her I will make sure you know his
wrath. They move aside, Tyndareus' name moves everyone
aside. I don't dare bury her in the royal grounds. I find a
remote grove and lay the pitiful babe to rest. I mark it well so
we can find her in better times should they ever come. And
the worst of it, the day, beautiful, such a sky. And the child,
eyes closed for all of time against these ordinary wonders.

SCENE TEN

Mycenae. Outside. Black sky. Stars.

Agamemnon Trouble afoot. All the tribes up in arms, the
islands raiding and slaughtering each other on the beaches
and in the hills, four of my trading ships lost to piracy.
They're trying to flush me out. Aegisthus egging them on.
An orphan girl sacrificed in the mountains to win fair words

from Delphi. Bulls offered on the shore. Two thousand men gathered, singing, dancing, kniving, Aegisthus strutting his stuff on the altars, the smell of roasting meat carrying for miles on the wind. And Delphi speaks. Of course Delphi speaks. Delphi speaks through the cracked lips of Colchis, the old whore. And what does Delphi say? Delphi says that Agamemnon is not the rightful king. Delphi says that Agamemnon is an upstart ingrate. And who is the rightful king? Aegisthus of course. And the little prophetess is afraid and the babes grow and it seems I must take up arms, drag this carcass up on old Aetha, thunder across the kingdom mustering men, get the fleets ready, go warring again.

Tyndareus I arrive at night, Mycenae lit up like a thousand suns. The golden lions at the gates, the gleaming road to the palace steps, cypress, elm, on either side playing hide and seek with the stars. He's at the ebony door waiting for me, arms folded, mouth set. He knows why I'm here. He gives the expected welcome but his heart's not in it. I've lived too long, only natural these young bucks want me to move over in the bed, give them a whirl at the top. He takes me to the inner hall, clears the room with a wave of his hand. The cup bearers pour and fill my plate.

Agamemnon He pushes the plates aside, fixes me with the gorgon stare he inherited from his mother.

Tyndareus Where is my daughter?

Agamemnon Tyndareus, I tried everything.

Tyndareus I'm not interested in what you tried.

Agamemnon I see fear in his eyes. This ancient who has ruled from the north to the western sea for sixty winters. This trembling old king, who in his prime led great armies, brought cities to their knees, left gilded monuments of himself all over the known world.

Tyndareus Where is she?

Agamemnon I've put her aside, I've put her to the harem.

Tyndareus You may send word now her father is come and will speak with her. No daughter of mine will be flung aside while I have a roof over my head.

Agamemnon I'm letting her cool off, let her remember who I am. I'll release her in my own time. This is a domestic matter, none of your concern.

Tyndareus My granddaughter Leda? Where is she?

Agamemnon With her mother.

Tyndareus You'll bring her to me now.

Agamemnon You'll give her to Aegisthus.

Tyndareus And if I do?

Agamemnon She'll stay with her mother.

Tyndareus You're cutting it very fine to treat any of mine in this manner. I took you in, a frightened boy running for your life. Have you forgotten that?

Agamemnon I haven't forgotten.

Tyndareus Reared you like one of my own, taught you everything I know about arts of war and arts of peace, led an army up to these very walls to get you back your birthright and your kingdom. I gave you my daughter. And now you think to throw her to the foot soldiers? My daughter?

Agamemnon You don't know what I've put up with.

Tyndareus And the word is the Trojan slave is now your queen?

Agamemnon And if she is?

Tyndareus Have you lost it entirely? Have you gone too high to heed your own people? They won't have it. And neither will I.

Agamemnon I've heard the word all right, Tyndareus. You and Aegisthus and every trumped-up cattle dealer who wants to be king. I've heard all about your new coalition. I'll see you in the field if you're fool enough to make a war over your daughter.

Tyndareus Give her back her rightful place and I'll sort out Aegisthus and his wide boys.

Agamemnon I told you, she won't have me.

Tyndareus You're not the first man ever spurned by a woman. I don't give a tinker's curse what's happening or not happening between your sheets. Just make it look like it is. You've the place in uproar, they'll take you out.

Agamemnon And you with them.

Tyndareus You know how delicate it all hangs. A lot of bad blood over the Trojan skirmish, too many lost, went on too long, war can only last a season, if I taught you nothing I taught you that. Put the Trojan lassie aside, stop this foolishness, I'll keep them at bay.

Agamemnon She hates me. She wants me dead.

Tyndareus Give her time. She has a lot to forgive.

Agamemnon She's out of control. You spoilt her, Tyndareus, spoilt her for any man. A heartless vindictive witch is what you've reared, merciless, expert in sluttery. I don't know about you but I like my woman soft.

Tyndareus Iphigenia! A child, Agamemnon! A girl child! Your own child! My grandchild! You have broken our hearts. An act of such savagery I still wake at night reeling. You've brought shame on our heads. It'll be a long time before the tribe forget. If ever. This is the age of bronze. We're not stone men from the caves. We don't sacrifice children on altars for winds to change. Is it any wonder she won't have you? How could she? On your knees before her you should be. On your knees till the day you die and that wouldn't be long enough.

I'm going into the old palace now to get my daughter and my granddaughter and you just try to stop me. it grieves me sore it has come to this but nothing decent ever came out of this house. You can plaster your walls in jade and mother of pearl, prance your floors of marble and stolen gold, but you're a savage from a long line of them. Your time is done. The future can't afford you.

SCENE ELEVEN

Sparta. Interior. Light different.

Clytemnestra I'm back in the rooms I had as a girl. My mother wanders in, a little bird with her gone away eyes. Who are you, she says, you look familiar. Then Helen is there with her daughter Hermione. And Helen says, they couldn't find Leda when they brought you from the old palace. I tell her that Leda is dead. My little niece Hermione cries and Helen takes her away. My father stands in the doorway giving orders.

Orestes. Electra. Bring them here because I fear for them now.

Tyndareus Rest, girl, rest.

I don't tell her that Agamemnon is too strong for us, has bribed and cajoled a new coalition and we must bide our time.

Rest, get your health again, he won't harm them.
I thought that one time too, she says, and turns her face away so I don't see her grief.

Cassandra I'm moved from the queen's apartments.
I haven't seen my infants though I keep asking for them to be brought. Agamemnon keeps away. I hear snippets, he's gone east, he's in Crete, he's making treaties with the

islands. I wander the palace, make my way to his wing but I'm stopped in the outer chamber though I can see him within. He looks through me as if I am not there, displeasure in his gaze, in full battle armour, his generals around him, maps on the floor, piles of gold on the tables, slave girls attending. I hear their laughter as I walk away.

Cilissa Electra is sent up country into the care of Agamemnon's mother's people. I'm forbidden to speak with Orestes. He trains with the other boys all day and sleeps in his father's chamber because Agamemnon fears he will be taken by Tyndareus or Aegisthus and his allies. There is a rout every day, skirmishes along the borders that escalate savagely, the barber surgeons exhausted in their blood-spattered aprons and funerals by the hour, young men carried on their shields for hasty burial, deserters and cowards hung in chains from the outer walls alongside the butchered enemy, some of them hardly more than children. The palace is a war factory, full to bursting with tribes from far flung places, swanking and preening, terrifying the slave women, Agamemnon tries to control their ferocity, stringing a few rapists up as deterrent, but most of their law breaking towards the slaves goes unpunished. The harem is unlocked and unguarded, free for all whenever they choose. The blood is up, the war god in their veins again. And again it is ugly. I keep my head covered when I go abroad but mostly I stay in my nook behind the empty nursery. And it's there he finds me.

Agamemnon I want you to ready her apartments as they were before. I want everything exactly as she left it. Can you do that?

Cilissa I can.

Agamemnon Where did you bury Leda?

Cilissa I did it for my lady.

Agamemnon Just tell me where you put the girl.

Cilissa In the callow, the grove there.

Agamemnon Could you find her grave?

Cilissa It's well marked.

Agamemnon I want you to dig her up and bury her again in the sacred grounds. Can you do that for me?

Cilissa I can.

Agamemnon Under cover of dark. All the offerings, flowers, make it look nice.

Cilissa Nice?

Agamemnon Yes, nice, Cilissa. It must look nice. God knows I'm sorry for the child to be caught up like this in her mother's mess. Between the jigs and the reels your precious mistress has the kingdom on its knees.

And I leave her before she speaks out of turn and I have to strike her down.

SCENE TWELVE

Exterior. Artemis' shore. Roar of the sea. Blue blue sky.

Clytemnestra Aegisthus prancing round my father's lands with his army. I'm dressed and put on a horse and follow the bulls and the bull runners who dance and somersault on the running herds. Two days' hard riding takes us to Artemis' shore and we make camp on the beach. Agamemnon's camp is on the cliff, can see his tent, flags flying in the breeze, euphoria in the air, the men out of their minds with anticipation as they build the altars and set the fires. My father huffing along the tide line giving orders.

Agamemnon They swagger below us hurling insults and high talk. I do a tally and see we're evenly matched. If it was by sea I'd have them to heel in a few light-hearted hours and this they know and look on in consternation as my black ships sail out of the blue and line up on the horizon. I hope not to use them but no harm to have them there. Battles being mostly won before a drop of blood is shed. Tyndareus knows this. Didn't he teach me himself? Aegisthus thrashing up and down the shore waving her colours, whooping and bragging this time tonight he'll have her in his bed and me in my grave. We'll see about that. I'm wearing her scarves too, close to my breast, habit, superstition, I've worn them since I was ten and first in the field. All this for a faithless jade past her prime. I tell Atarxis to start the slaughter of the bulls. The chants begin, the charlatans from Delphi, working the men till they roar and sing above the screaming beasts. I could do without this fracas. The kingdom can't afford it. We were just getting on our feet after Troy and it scuppers my great visions of exploring further east. But they want rid of me. See it everywhere I go. My faults? Just the one. I'm too good at what I do. Orestes by my side, his heart in his face as he looks on. I leap on the altar as they bring the first bull. The priests robe me, daub and slather me in the sacred oils. I put on the mask, take the sacrificial knife, twist the neck, bring it to its knees and slit the sweating throat. The men roar, weep, stamp, Zeus Agamemnon, Zeus Agamemnon. I fling my arms skyward where they'd have us believe the gods lean down to watch. I rip out the bull's still beating heart and offer it to the invisible. The men, as usual, go wild, fight over the testicles and first cup of blood. All the altars are at it now. In a while the air will be black with smoke and they'll feast on the meat till they're sick. I go to my tent, fling off the robes, down a cup of wine. Age of gold, age of bronze, what does it matter, tomorrow we'll destroy one another on a whim, what we're here for it seems.

Cassandra Mycenae is empty. I search the women's quarters for my babes and come upon Clytemnestra's slave in the queen's rooms. She is folding and perfuming robes from the vast wardrobe.

Cilissa Who gave you permission to enter here?

Cassandra I can't find my infants and no one tells me anything.

Cilissa And though she is my lady's rival and enemy, I feel sorry for this girl who never abused her position when she was high and now is surely lost.

Agamemnon has sent them for safety to his mother's people.

Cassandra Will I ever see them again?

Cilissa Do I wear the crown? Don't be stupid, we're just their playthings.

Cassandra But my children.

Cilissa Your children? What about my children? Don't talk to me about children.

SCENE THIRTEEN

Artemis' shore.

Aegisthus Dawn. Haze on the waves. The camps stirring. We breakfast on diluted wine and barley cakes. Armour donned. Horses galloping in the surf, flags flying, naked foot soldiers with their cheap spears, their shields of goat skin that wouldn't stop a new dropped fawn not to mind the Walusian savages and the golden elite of the Carians. The Dorians.

Tyndareus The Dorians. The Ahhawayians, the Vistuxians, the Boroi, the Thebans with their masks of hammered gold and jewelled scimitars. I get up on my horse and sweat in my robes of rust. Agamemnon on old Aetha, moving calmly among his men, the black ships with their prows to the east as if they're only dawdling, the slaves sweeping up the bones, carcasses, skulls of the slaughtered bulls, raking the sand, combing it flat for the battle ahead, the Scythians prancing, the Assyrians dour and still.

Clytemnestra Orestes comes towards me surrounded by Agamemnon's boon companions and my heart turns in its chains to see my beautiful boy in his miniature armour, sword on his hip, the bare brown feet. Your lord and king commands your return. His voice even, calm, the eyes faraway. I want to take him in my arms but that would shame him, his first battlefield. Orestes, I say, surely you're not fighting today? My father comes, lays his hand on my son's head.

Tyndareus Now my gorgeous knave, go back and tell your pappi, he has pulled on our heartstrings too long. Clytemnestra stays here.

And I kiss his blessed head. What a proud little fellow. You could bring him anywhere. They got that much right.

Agamemnon First the foot soldiers whirling like fire, whooping, leaping, falling on each other, the sound deafening, flesh ripped open, limbs hanging, the cries desperate, the dying groans, the terrible weeping, the sand a midden of blood and entrails. No one is sure who has won this bout, so close it is. A pause is demanded to count the dead, hotly disputed, tempers raging, shoving, cursing, jostling. Each side roaring they are the victors, though I'm sure we have the advantage but they hate me so much now they will not concede. Then the Scythians with their tattooed faces come in against our golden Mycenaean elite.

Clytemnestra Glimpses of him as the battle rages. It seems as if he moves in slow motion among them through the emerald morning. He appears, disappears, stretcher bearers running in and out of the fray, dragging the wounded to the surgeons' tents. I can't see Orestes. The stink of sweat, metal, blood, not a puff of wind, the waves coming silent to the shore.

Aegisthus Scythians gaining on Agamemnon's elite, dirty, ferocious, both sides call in reserves, the beach a rainbow of all the different tribes.

Agamemnon Battlefields are like women. This one harder to win than I thought. We'll get there but murderous slog in this heat. Young men who've hardly fought before, they stand there, doe eyed, shaking, no grace, no joy in cutting them down and still they keep coming, I slash and mow, get the rhythm, lose track of time.

Tyndareus We call in the boy armies. Their slaughter is desperate, children running with their guts in their hands, chased down by the horses, some into the sea where they flail and drown, wailing for their fathers, their mothers. Agamemnon is gaining, pushing our men back beyond the lines. The black ships start rowing in.

Aegisthus There's a pause. Agamemnon has fallen. No. Can it be? No. Tyndareus. Tyndareus is down. His men surround him as the Argives move in for the kill. Many more gifted than me have sung the bravery and beauty of the battlefield. I've never understood what it is they found to praise. But watching Tyndareus' men surround him as he lies bleeding on the sand, fighting blindly to keep them off, is a thing to behold. Agamemnon rides up, commands them to fall back, insists on safe passage for Tyndareus. Easy for him to do this. The battle is over. Everyone knows it. Agamemnon is victor again. Bad cess to him. Lady Luck smiling on him for the thousandth time. We gather our wounded, finish off the hopeless, set the pyres alight to burn the dead, wash ourselves in the sea.

Clytemnestra They carry my father through the stricken men already beating their breasts and singing their laments. I follow them to his tent, flapping white, flapping gold. They strip him as he roars with the pain. The barber surgeons put him flat on his back and go to work.

Come on, Pappi, you've survived worse.

My old father weeps when they come for me, kisses me, blesses me. We won't meet again this side of the grave, he says. Atarxis and his men lead me away and once we're out of my father's sight they put me in chains.

SCENE FOURTEEN

Mycenae. Interior.

Cilissa She arrives alongside the common prisoners. I hardly recognise her as she files past, hands chafed, face scalded by the sun, her feet in tatters.

Clytemnestra Three days' walk from Artemis' shore. The tribe come out to stare as I pass, glad to see me brought low, my reign over, Agamemnon's wayward wife getting her comeuppance. In the courtyard Cilissa runs to me but the soldiers push her away and escort me to Agamemnon's wing. The men high on their victory, drinking, gaming, singing, groping the serving girls who move among them with pitchers of wine and trays of meat. The curtain is drawn aside to the inner sanctum. He's in his silver bath, the little prophetess beside him. The big arrogant face, sloshing and dousing, the tyrant lip, the scowl when he sees me. He nods and the guards walk me through to the sacred presence.

Agamemnon There she is, battered from the road. That'll put manners on her.

Clytemnestra Sit, he says, and clicks his fingers and my shackles are taken off. The Trojan girl stares. A goblet appears in my hand.

Agamemnon Don't worry, I'm finished with you. Well finished.

Clytemnestra It's me who's finished with you.

Agamemnon I'm the one who says when it's finished.

61

Clytemnestra Leda?

Agamemnon Children are their mother's job. You should've looked after her better. I thought to grow old with you, count the grey blossoms on our heads, get fat, drink wine, I thought to have your arms around me, the last face I'd see, I thought to have you with me till the end but you've robbed us of that.

Clytemnestra I've robbed us?

Agamemnon Your stupid pride, your heartless judgement where you've no right to judge. Did no one ever tell you the sweetest revenge is to forgive? But I'm wasting my breath because no matter what I say or do, you look at me and all you see, all you want to see, is a girl on an altar.

Clytemnestra Do you remember the day she was born?

Agamemnon What I remember and don't remember won't save you now.

Clytemnestra The pains started before dawn. You were lying beside me. You said, I hope it's a girl. You said, I want only girls. Girls like you. And when she was born you rushed in, took her from the midwives, covered her in kisses, held her up naked to the sun. And I thought how lucky she is, he will be her great protector as he is mine. You held her up to the sun to bless her, our little princess of Argos. You held her up to the sun and prayed that nothing, nothing would ever harm her. And now Leda. Is there anything of mine you won't destroy?

Agamemnon You're wrong as you're wrong about everything. I was fond of the child.

Clytemnestra You put up with her as long as you thought you could bring me to heel. You allowed her live as long as I toed the line. But the second I refused you, you threw us to the wolves.

Agamemnon I'm going to hang you in chains in front of your precious children.

Clytemnestra Do that.

Cassandra She flings the goblet aside and takes up an axe that's lying among a pile of spears, maces, daggers. The Lydian two-bladed axe. She turns, looks at him. He looks at her in disbelief as she fingers the edge. You want my love, she says, here it is, here's all you understand, here's all my love. You wouldn't dare, he says but she's charging, arms high, he tries to get out of the bath but she's on him, a frenzy of blood and blade, the first blow nearly decapitates him, he falls roaring as she swings and strikes, swings and strikes.

Agamemnon Is she whispering? What's she whispering? The little prophetess hovers. So this is what it comes down to. An axe, a raging wife, a bath. Are you satisfied now, woman? Are we even? All right between us again?

Cassandra And then, as foretold, she comes for me.

Music.
End.